Love...without Distance

J.J. Villan

BookLeaf Publishing

India | USA | UK

Dedication

I do not write for
the perfect women
with the perfect lives

who do not know
of struggle
of heartache
of loss
of poverty
of sacrifice
of disappointment
or of tragedy

All life has ever given to me is
the gift of wisdom
forged by pain

I write for women like me
those who have been broken gracefully

The phoenixes who learn to rise
from their ashes
and do not choose
to stay destroyed by them

Qierra "Yoshie" White
I dedicate this collection to you

A girl who saw love
in everyone
And everything

Continue to stretch your wings
and rise in heaven queen

Preface

This is a prequel of poems from my
upcoming book Through the Soul & Out

This selection of poems is for the
anxious lover girls of the world
who let our emotions and passions
guide us on our journeys

Our unfolding paths
led by the compass of
our wild and curious hearts

May we all learn to find comfort in our
inner-gy -- (energy),
stay grounded in our power,
and never shy away from the
seasons where we grow
in our solitude

I hope we continue to keep
our hearts pure and postures upright
even if it means sometimes
we must collect some scars along the way

Cheers,
to forever staying
kind yet assertive,
gentle and strong,
all in the name
of finding and embodying
the true essence of
unconditional love

I pray you learn your boundaries
choose to love yourselves fully
and go after all your wildest dreams!

With Love,
J.J. Villan

Acknowledgements

Thank you to everyone that has supported me on this journey of stepping into myself as a writer and poet. I have finally found the courage to let my voice be heard and I hope these poems land in the hands of those that need them most.

If you find yourself broken and searching for a piece of poetry that resonates with you on your own healing journey I hope you find it here. I feel you, I am with you, I was you, I am you. We are in this together. Please believe that with faith anything is possible including overcoming whatever challenges, heartbreaks, grief, or loss you maybe feeling.
Know that you are loved.

1. What is love

She asked the poet:
How would you describe falling in love?

You mean,
the feeling of skydiving
without a parachute?

The risky chance of both
floating or crashing?

The leap of faith
that we blindly take
in hope of catching joy
in the palm of our hands
like rain water,
knowing that we take on
the dangerous possibility
of caressing lightning instead?

The adrenaline rush of it all

not knowing how long the fall will last
but isn't it still a beautiful dream?
Knowing that we may open up a heart
and call it home,
paint its walls with our laughs,
even if just for the moment?

Until the broken promises
that were once spoken during
the honey moon season
retreat back into the
grottoes of our throats,
and the butterflies
decide to hibernate in our bellies,
until the next one shakes the core of us
and awakens our curiosity
and fascination once more.

Love said the poet,
Is the nature in us
stretching to sunrise
to take on an unwritten day
that begins with a potent expresso shot
of hope desire and wonder.

It is what we make it and want it to be
just so long as we are willing to

have the courage to nurture
and explore it continuously,
and when it no longer
wants to be claimed
we care for it so much

we choose to set it free....

2. Love Song

I can still recall when you
made my body into a harp
you played me with your fingertips
pulled every string in me
until I became
a love song

3. Midnight Fever

When I am around them
my stomach turns dishwasher
and I can still feel all the fragile fine china
that consist of my awkwardness and shyness
loudly clanking inside of me

I wonder if they know
I am one laugh away
from shattering in their presence

The introverted side of me left in pieces
as my confidence sweeps in to finally say
more words than a simple hello

My courage a dustpan on standby
waiting to catch my anxiety as it slowly
starts to slip from my frame

Our shoulders barely graze
the hairs on the back of my neck

stand at attention as if they are
small soldiers saluting their aura

They make me nervous
tickle my jitter bugs
in a good kind of a way
instead of stretching their wings
to take flight
they start to relax

I look up at the night sky
take notice to the crescent moon
smiling back at me
matching my own grin that
has now settled on my face

I think to myself
I just might stay

A little while longer

4. Colliding Paradise

My favorite part of our days
has become leaving the house together
waiting for the anticipation of when
we find our way back to this kiss
where a hesitant goodbye transforms
into an excited "Hello!"
and an enduring "Be safe"
changes to a soothing
"How was your day?"

Where we make our way
to the cave of the bedroom
bodies puzzle pieced together
connecting our souls
with the hopes of the moonlight
caressing our silhouettes
through the wooden shutters
and small windows

Until the first rays of dawn

stretches its limbs to reach out
and plant a gentle kiss
upon each of our foreheads
as I ease into a sleeping beauty slumber
in the hammock of your arms

Late nights early mornings
days running together
time nonexistent
with our smiles
reflecting off the windshield
during our car rides

My favorite part of our days is leaving
finger tips releasing
each others grasp
until we can again
make our way
back down that dirt road
on this floating rock
in the middle of the Caribbean Sea

Into that driveway
through the threshold
of a place where we have found momentary peace
in between the chaos of our colliding worlds

Creating a temporary home made in each others
embrace
discovering that this islands magic can brings two land
like bodies
so close together that they merge into its own paradise

My favorite part of my day is you

5. Mirror Mirror

The things we had to lose in order to climb this high
And rise to this kind of frequency
To find each other
On this timeline
Until we finally aligned
It was first harshly tragic
Somehow
It had to be turned upside down
Until all was soft and beautiful
————————————————————
Until all was soft and beautiful
It had to be turned upside down
Somehow
It was first harshly tragic
Until we finally aligned
On this timeline
To find each other
And rise to this kind of frequency
The things we had to lose in order to climb this high

6. Favorite Place

I want my heart to be well traveled
when I reach the end of this life's journey
I want the dirt embedded on
the outsoles of my shoes
telling its own story

Each grain of sand a honorable mention
each scuff a kind reminder of past adventures
of all the places where my feet has taken the lead
and my heart dared to blindly follow

Down the roadways that directed me
to the bank of your smile,
where I have bathed privately
in the river of your love
It has been the greatest location to learn and explore

I built a house out of the good
bones of our most intimate moments
There it still stands at the fork road of

Meant-to-be Street and Forget-Me-Not Lane

I hung pictures of us all over its walls
turned our secrets we shared into vinyl
to play when I want to feel close to you
and fall for you all over again

Reciting the lines to all of our
Silly sweet nothings we used to whisper
Replaying the time we would wrestle
And lock our lanky limbs
into chains on that bed

Your scent still potent enough to smell vividly
through the seams of our crocheted memories
A mixture between your cologne and the ocean
that crashed against the Malecón across the street

When we are long gone
And nothing more than ashes
gifted back to the earth
I want my soul to remember
that I was once well traveled
and my legs did not forget
the voyage of which they had to trek
in order to find the point of when
I first discovered your name

Because in every lifetime that I have come to live
You have always been my favorite place

7. Pull

My darling you are magnetic
You make every fragment
that is left of
this heart of steel ....

dance for you

8. Wishing Well

She held the entire ocean within her frame
I can tell by the depth in her eyes
her soul had so much of a story to say

My heart wanted to hold all of her secrets
like they were coins being gifted
to the well of me

Her words flowed like water
there is no thirst hidden
between the lines
of her poetry

9. Love unrequited

Karma,
the carousel ride
of unrequited love

The only way to end the
haunting push and pull thrill
is to hop off the trauma cycle
and finally decide to heal

Karma,
the chaotic rotation of
be hurt to cause hurt
to be hurt again
the still holding onto the past
when something new tries to begin

Karma,
the what you put out
is what you get back
the emotionally unavailable

causing relationships
to be unstable
as they play the game
of catch a new match

make them attach
pull away
discard
run away
detach

Karma,
a loop of the blues
patterns on queue to repeat
where the naive girls lose
and the soft girls weep

10. Soul Scars

How many times have you recalled
a knife kissing the wound
and telling it sorry after it
causes a gash?

Most scars are forced to close alone after all,
some with no assistance

I have come to the acceptance
You were the love turned blade
and the cuts you made
may never heal
and apologies
may never come

11. Sacrifice

"Do not take it personal"
my mind told my heart

At some point in time
we are all called
to the front line
to be a casualty
in this war of love

Our hearts just a sacrifice
for the progression
of another's self growth

Before the love bomb drops
and the lies detonate
onto the next woman
that comes to take my place

I hope she is able to hear
the faint cries that hide

in between your
tear stained sheets
and feels the heat

of all the hearts
that burned there
before hers

12. Warzone

This body be a gun
waiting to discharge

anxiety being the one bullet
that is left in the chamber
depression being the trigger

I have become a weapon
filled with my own destruction
the worst thing I have come to fear
is being held in another's possession

afraid that they will fail
to handle me with care
when my patience is not
always set on safety

anticipating their mouth to be the fire
that may ignite the gun powder
that causes my impulsive explosion

we all know how the shooter
is the one that loves to blame
the firearm for the casualties
but we also know it is really
hurt people who hurt people

as if to say
that we are all capable
of becoming arsenal
in the wrong set of hands

this world being a holster
as we are carried on life's hip
afraid of the day where we may
be drawn on each other
letting off rounds with our words
creating more wounds that
others are left to heal from

It's sad when life has come to be
just a battlefield
where even love
becomes the warzone

13. Dragons

Dragons sleep in the belly of your rage
you spit fire with your words

and wonder why there is nothing left
to salvage in the end

14. Fickle Fire

Pretty girl
do not be tempted
to tend to fickle fires
that burn in the furnace of your heart
but do not have the intention
of ever bringing warmth to your entire soul

15. Splinters

I am not afraid of love
I am however terrified of people

of their intentions
of how they are capable
of destruction and radical change

of how they can take
strong standing trees of women
and chop them down
until they are nothing more

than mere splinters
left searching for their roots

16. Plucked Petals

As much as I thought I had healed
I soon would learn that your
hands would pluck
every insecurity in me
until my body became a rose
with no petals left to sacrifice

she loves me
she loves me not

17. Thorns

Do not fear your tears
the soul said to the broken heart
they are not weakness leaving the body
they are simply taking their exit
to allow more strength to fill you to the brim

Does water not help the rose sprout its thorns
to pluck the hands that try to uproot
it from its foundation ?

Let them fall

And although it may be painful
now is the time to embrace your thorns
and love all the piercing parts of you

18. Saving grace

I have learned
Love does not flee
When you are depleted and weak
With no water left to spare

Instead love says
Hold on a little longer
I am strong enough for the both of us
To survive the drought that has found us here

The cactus kissed the desert
while it was cracking in pain
The clouds bared witness to its devotion
And released its tears of rain
Down pouring enough love
For the both of them to be relieved
of their suffering
restoring their vitality

This is a blessing
This is saving grace

19. locked heart

My soul gently whispered
Do not lock away your heart
It is my favorite part of you

20. Weeping Willow

When does the weeping willow finally meet bliss
When it is greeted by a firm hug, kind words, and gentle
kiss

Its tears turn to nectar
when it learns to love its roots
and it finally gives its branches permission
to lean into their droop

A weeping willow tree finds joy
when it submits and has every intent
to be free
and learns it needs to be nothing more
than a magnificent willow tree

when it no longer feels the need to be
embarrassed by its own display
and it embraces why god made it
exactly that way

Its unruly nature a constant reminder
that it's beauty is not to be defined
by those who can not see why
it is one of a kind

The weeping willow finally gets to giggle
when it accepts the truth of it being
the center piece of the scene
and the wanderers perfect find
a place for lovers to rest their eyes
and etch their initials along her spine

When she realizes that
she is gods good humor
is when she can finally begin to laugh
the tree that makes God crack his smile back

He waits like a gentle father
for her to realize the lesson
That she is indeed
the diamond in the swamp
the gardens sweet blessing

21. Butterfly beginnings

Let go
the cocoon told the butterfly while wrapping it in one
final embrace
It is time to spread your wings and show all your colors
to the world
you are the evidence of how god creates miracles and
can transform us all
into something more beautiful with patience and faith

even if we can not yet see for ourselves
all that we are destined to become
the caterpillar did not sneak into the sheathe
of me and expect my hug to have so much love
and believe that I could make it fly one day

but here you are as majestic as ever
the proof that sometimes crawling into the unknown and
uncomfortable spaces
is what is needed to grow strength
so go now spread your wings

and give someone else the gift of hope

Let your flight
be the path they find themselves
following
to lead them into
their own new beginning

www.ingramcontent.com/pod-product-compliance
Lightning Source LLC
LaVergne TN
LVHW010915200726
843509LV00013B/1953